First World War
and Army of Occupation
War Diary
France, Belgium and Germany

21 DIVISION
63 Infantry Brigade,
Brigade Machine Gun Company
1 March 1916 - 31 July 1916

WO95/2158/5

The Naval & Military Press Ltd
www.nmarchive.com
Published in association with The National Archives

Published by

The Naval & Military Press Ltd

Unit 10 Ridgewood Industrial Park,

Uckfield, East Sussex,

TN22 5QE England

Tel: +44 (0) 1825 749494

www.naval-military-press.com

www.nmarchive.com

This diary has been reprinted in facsimile from the original. Any imperfections are inevitably reproduced and the quality may fall short of modern type and cartographic standards.

© **Crown Copyright**
Images reproduced by permission of The National Archives, London, England, 2015.

Contents

Document type	Place/Title	Date From	Date To
Miscellaneous	WO95/2158/5		
Heading	21st Division 63rd Infy Bde 63rd Machine Gun Coy. Mar-Jly 1916 To 37 Div		
Heading	War Diary of 63rd Inft brigade machine gun company from 1st March 1916 to 31st March 1916 volume 1		
War Diary	Havre	01/03/1916	03/03/1916
War Diary	Steenverch	03/03/1916	04/03/1916
War Diary	Armentieres	04/03/1916	21/03/1916
War Diary	La Creeche	21/03/1916	22/03/1916
War Diary	Strazeele	22/03/1916	31/03/1916
Miscellaneous	Memorandum.	29/05/1916	29/05/1916
War Diary	Pradelles	01/04/1916	08/04/1916
War Diary	Buire	09/04/1916	09/04/1916
War Diary	Ville.	10/04/1916	17/04/1916
War Diary	Meault.	18/04/1916	22/04/1916
War Diary	Ville	23/04/1916	23/04/1916
War Diary	Bonnay	24/04/1916	03/05/1916
War Diary	Ville	03/05/1916	12/05/1916
War Diary	Meault	12/05/1916	22/05/1916
War Diary	Ville.	23/05/1916	23/05/1916
War Diary	La Neuville	23/05/1916	02/06/1916
War Diary	Ville	03/06/1916	10/06/1916
War Diary	Ville to Meault	11/06/1916	20/06/1916
War Diary	Ville	20/06/1916	20/06/1916
War Diary	La Neuville	21/06/1916	30/06/1916
Miscellaneous	Memorandum.	31/07/1916	31/07/1916
War Diary	Fricourt	30/06/1916	04/07/1916
War Diary	Dernancourt	04/07/1916	04/07/1916
War Diary	Vaux	05/07/1916	07/07/1916
War Diary	Grenas	08/07/1916	11/07/1916
War Diary	Bienvillers	12/07/1916	14/07/1916
War Diary	Humbercamp	15/07/1916	15/07/1916
War Diary	Houvigneul.	16/07/1916	16/07/1916
War Diary	Guestreville	17/07/1916	18/07/1916
War Diary	Chateau De La Haye	18/07/1916	25/07/1916
War Diary	Camblain L'Abbe.	26/07/1916	27/07/1916
War Diary	Cabaret Rouge.	28/07/1916	31/07/1916

3095 / 2158 / 5

21ST DIVISION
63RD INFY BDE

63RD MACHINE GUN COY.
MAR - JLY 1916

To 37 DIV

21ST DIVISION
63RD INFY BDE

ORIGINAL

21st Div 63.
63 Inf
Bde MG
Coy
Vol 1

CONFIDENTIAL

WAR DIARY

OF

63rd Inft Brigade Machine Gun Company

FROM 1st MARCH 1916 TO 31st MARCH 1916

VOLUME 1

Army Form C. 2118.

WAR DIARY
or
INTELLIGENCE SUMMARY.
(Erase heading not required.)

Instructions regarding War Diaries and Intelligence Summaries are contained in F.S. Regs., Part II. and the Staff Manual respectively. Title pages will be prepared in manuscript.

Place	Date	Hour	Summary of Events and Information	Remarks and references to Appendices
HAVRE	1-3-16		No special orders received today. Re-supply of coy transpt.	SD v fs
HAVRE	2-3-16	9 AM	Order received that coy transp had arrived	
		11 AM	Order received that 1 & 2nd coy would entrain at HAVRE-GARE MARCHANDISE at 6.30 AM - to start 12 MN	SD v fs
		9.41 PM	1st coy movement to Turnpike Station	1 D v fb
HAVRE	3-3-16	2 AM	Placed 1/2 of the coy moved out of the station.	
STEENWERCK		6.30 PM	1st & 2nd coy arrived at STEENWERCK & march to billets in ARMENTIERES	SD v fs
STEENWERCK	4-3-16	2 AM	2nd & 3rd coy arrived at ARMENWERCK STATION & marched to billets in ARMENTIERES	
ARMENTIERES		11 AM	Order received to reconn. line that coy will take over.	SD v fs
ARMENTIERES	5-3-16	10 AM	Orders received that 3 sections would take over positions line	
"		3 PM	Positions taken over. Coy HQ established in CHAPELLE ARMENTIERES	SD v fs
"	6-3-16		No order received. Positions inspected by day sought little shelling v snowing	SD v fs
"	7-3-16		Nothing special today.	SD v fs
"	8-3-16		Considerable amount of work done in making new emplacements etc.	SD v fs

WAR DIARY
INTELLIGENCE SUMMARY
(Erase heading not required.)

Army Form C. 2118.

Instructions regarding War Diaries and Intelligence Summaries are contained in F. S. Regs., Part II. and the Staff Manual respectively. Title pages will be prepared in manuscript.

Place	Date	Hour	Summary of Events and Information	Remarks and references to Appendices
B.H.Q. EQUIHEN	8.3.16		Considerable amount of work done on emplacements. Not enough men in the Coy to do required work	SD v. P.B.
"	9.3.16		Coy spread to night ------	SD v. P.B.
"	10.3.16		Little ------ during the day. Work done on emplacements ------	SD v. P.B.
"	11.3.16		Coy absented to night during the day	
"			------ carried out at night	SD v. P.B.
"	12.3.16		No ------ Considerable amount of work done on emplacements.	SD v. P.B.
"			------ fire at night ------	SD v. P.B.
"	13.3.16		No ------ during the night ------	
"	14.3.16		9.30 a.m. enemy withdrew a horse standing by his State. Repeats afterwards by 1/2 Bn. ------	SD v. P.B.
"			Wire ------ to day on emplacements. Working parties ------ at night	
"	15.3.16		------ to ------	SD v. P.B.
"			------ being ------ we find it ------ to use any the German machine guns active	SD v. P.B.
"			to night ------ ------ ------	

Army Form C. 2118.

WAR DIARY
or
INTELLIGENCE SUMMARY.
(Erase heading not required.)

Instructions regarding War Diaries and Intelligence Summaries are contained in F. S. Regs., Part II. and the Staff Manual respectively. Title pages will be prepared in manuscript.

Place	Date	Hour	Summary of Events and Information	Remarks and references to Appendices
ARMENTIERES	17/3/16		Very quiet day. Just getting settled in billets.	SDV.BA
"	18/3/16		O.C. of Brigade Mg Company takes over all emplacements in our own Sub sector	SDV.BA
	19/3/16		Spun off 5000 rds by lately light over the emplacements during the morning	
		4 PM	One 1 NCO 2 Men with relieved by similar party of 15 Bn	
			Major returning the evening back to ARMENTIERES.	
			Six horses had to go at walk over to Lareveneil the kit away to be at sufficient transport	SDV.BA
				SDV.BA
				SDV.BA
			Orders received to move back to area	SDV.BA
	20/3/16	9 AM	Left ARMENTIERES 9 SAM. Marched to LA CRECHE	
LA CRECHE	21/3/16	12 MD	Arrived LA CRECHE. Billeted in Farms Nurot and Lanform afternoon.	
	22/3/16	8 AM	Left LA CRECHE area. Marched to STRAZEELE	
STRAZEELE		11 AM	Arrived STRAZEELE & STRAZEELE	SDV.BA
	23/3/16	5 PM	Orders received to move billets. This was immediately done	
		8 PM	Secured new billets.	1 DV BA
	24/3/16		Wet and gun during the day.	SDV.BA

WAR DIARY

INTELLIGENCE SUMMARY.

Army Form C. 2118.

Instructions regarding War Diaries and Intelligence Summaries are contained in F. S. Regs., Part II. and the Staff Manual respectively. Title pages will be prepared in manuscript.

(Erase heading not required.)

Place	Date	Hour	Summary of Events and Information	Remarks and references to Appendices
STRAZEELE	1.9.16		Gas demonstration in morning	
"	"		Was a quiet afternoon	
"	26.9.16		No official orders received	
"	27.9.16		Good progress of work	
"	28.9.16	10.30AM	O.C. this brigade inspects transport in afternoon	
"	29.9.16		Usual program of work & training	
"	"		Observation in afternoon. Orders to evacuate billets & to	
"	30.9.16		Strafflight - I.E. 4 hrs. look. Sent to brigade — owing to go in lorry.	
"	2.10.16 8PM	PARADE. MARCHED TO GDEWAERSUEIDE STATION	
"	1.10.16	NDPM	Arrived Station & entrained	

MEMORANDUM.

Army Form C. 348.

From 63 Machine Gun Coy

To D.A.G.
    Base.

From

To

ANSWER.

May 29th 1916.

Herewith war diary for the month of April. Any delay very much regretted

W. G. A. Coldwell Major
O.C. 63 Machine Gun Coy

Army Form C. 2118.

63 MG Coy
Vol 2

WAR DIARY
or
INTELLIGENCE SUMMARY
(Erase heading not required.)

Instructions regarding War Diaries and Intelligence Summaries are contained in F. S. Regs., Part II. and the Staff Manual respectively. Title pages will be prepared in manuscript.

Place	Date	Hour	Summary of Events and Information	Remarks and references to Appendices
PRADELLES	1st April	8.30 PM to 1.45 AM	March 3rd — Marched to GODEWAERSVELDE — entrained by 1 PM 2.4.16 Moved off 1.45 — The entraining being done quickly much — arrived LONGUEUX, 12.30 PM.	
	2nd		Detrained very quickly indeed — marched through AMIENS to ALLONVILLE, arrived there — 6.30 PM. Unpacked limbers — Usual performance of tools (harness corrected) — Other Coys had night for	
			section to proceed next day to BUIRE	
	3rd	6 AM	No 3 section paraded marched to BUIRE — training continued for remaining sections —	
	4th		No 3 section took over part of the trenches in front of ALBERT, transport of this section took over —	
	5th		Transport field of 97th Bde at DERNANCOURT —	
			Usual programme of work — sections billeted in Duchess's gables into which both limbers at a spot 1 mile distant — kept left hung open — well kept satisfactory —	
			Made rations improving under excellent weather conditions —	
	6th		Usual programme of work — Section formed in the trenches preparatory to moving to BUIRE.	
	7th	7.30	Coy paraded — marched with the Brigade to BUIRE — arriving 1 PM —	
			Games etc. cleaned down the afternoon	
	8th		OC 63 had orders to inspect the receding line in case of German attack — this line ran in Corbeau Wood 2.06 PM —	

WAR DIARY
or
INTELLIGENCE SUMMARY.
(Erase heading not required.)

Army Form C. 2118.

Place	Date	Hour	Summary of Events and Information	Remarks and references to Appendices
BUIRE	9th April		Coy moved to VILLE - 3/4 of a mile - Being Bank Holiday transport (which is a reserve question) the journey had to be made by our transport -	
VILLE	10th		O.C. Coys again inspected the total secondary line accompanied by section officers - Gun positions detailed to each section - transport tools reorganized -	
	11th	2 pm	Sections retired to a selected line -	
	12th	10 am	O.C. Coy & Coy officers visited positions prepared by sections in the line - rained all day -	
	13th		Went programme of work carried on - during the last 3 days the Coys was instructed in use of grenades.	
			" Issued of Nos 1, 2 & 4 Sections taken Bivouacs Brick dumps -	
	14th	7.30 pm	Preparatory to relieving 64th M.G. Coy - Sections paraded received by M.G. Coys - Coy Hd. No 3 sect moved to MEAULT - relief completed by noon - quiet day -	
	15th		Quiet day - 2 of our guns opened indirect fire by night - retaliation received - Enemy M. Guns - which suddenly turned	
	16th		Quiet day - some slight shelling - Indirect fire opened - FRICOURT Fm & WOOD - heavy hostile retaliation	
	17th		Enemy quiet - some shelling in CEMETERY R' SECTOR.	

Army Form C. 2118.

WAR DIARY
or
INTELLIGENCE SUMMARY.
(Erase heading not required.)

Instructions regarding War Diaries and Intelligence Summaries are contained in F. S. Regs., Part II. and the Staff Manual respectively. Title pages will be prepared in manuscript.

Place	Date	Hour	Summary of Events and Information	Remarks and references to Appendices
MEAULT.	18th		Desultory Enemy artillery fire most of the day - fired 185 rounds admitted Hospital both	
	19th		Spotted Enemy - I fired one to the G.S. Heavy bombardment of Combe sector - TAMBOUR vicinity - fire opened by 6" A. Guns at a raid was thought probable - no lull took place however - possibly in consequence of our M guns which were kept laid at night in the eventually of such attack.	
	20th	9.A.m	O.C. 6" Visited parts of the trenches with the G.O.C. 85th Bde. for the purpose of ascertaining various tactical requirements - Indirect fire opened by 66 hour and night into the valley between FRICOURT & MAMETZ. No new gun emplacements constructed -	
	21st		Quiet day - nothing to report - Much took place at night -	
	22nd		Enemy heavy artillery - relieved by 62 Hey. Co? - 62 marched back to VILLE station via old billets there -	
VILLE	23rd	11.A.m	62 moved off to BONNAY - arriving 1.15 P.m - Spotted two corporal + 1/Sto from Case -	
BONNAY	24th		62 carried back to all officers of the 6" visited - No 1,2,3 & 4 sections transferred Split up amongst the 4 Reg ts of the Brigade -	

Army Form C. 2118.

WAR DIARY
or
INTELLIGENCE SUMMARY.
(Erase heading not required.)

Instructions regarding War Diaries and Intelligence Summaries are contained in F. S. Regs., Part II. and the Staff Manual respectively. Title pages will be prepared in manuscript.

Place	Date	Hour	Summary of Events and Information	Remarks and references to Appendices
BINNAY.			No diary can be kept for the month of April - owing to the isolation of all officers except this inspector - 2/Lt Phillips admitted Hospital May 3rd (Jaundice). The various sections attached to various Reg.ts in the Brigade moved at LA NEUVILLE & carried on training & firing (practice).	

W. A. Coldwell Capt.
O.C. 63 Machine Gun Co.

Army Form C. 2118.

WAR DIARY
or
INTELLIGENCE SUMMARY.
(Erase heading not required.)

Instructions regarding War Diaries and Intelligence Summaries are contained in F. S. Regs., Part II. and the Staff Manual respectively. Title pages will be prepared in manuscript.

Place	Date	Hour	Summary of Events and Information	Remarks and references to Appendices
BONNAY	1st May		Officers of Coy + Coy H.Q. still billeted - see diary for April.	
	2nd May			
	3rd	12 noon	Had orders for Officers + Coy H.Q. (with Coy) proceed heavy [exposed?] to proceed to VILLE below. Nos 1,2,3,4 sections + Transport moved from us -	
VILLE		4.30	Officers + Coy H.Q. arrived VILLE, sections joined up with us and report billets in two minute again taken over -	
	4th		Through check of all gun equipt - stores etc -	
	5th		Used pouring hard - Requisite drill foo? particulars attention to -	
	6th		"	
	7th		Coy total - Church parade	
	8th		Nos 1 + 2 sections fired a practice shoot on the range at BUIRE	
	9th	2.30 pm	G.O.C. 63rd Inf Bde inspected the Coy + expressed his satisfaction - particularly with the Transport -	
	10th		Went Pozieres + took - practicing the Consolidation of positions N.C.O.s instructed in transport duties - Men told to be continued as opportunity arose -	
	11th		Usual work in billets	
	12th	5.45pm	Nos 1 3, 4 sections relieved 64 M.G. Coy in the line - No 2 section + Coy H.Q. proceeded to	

Army Form C. 2118.

WAR DIARY
or
INTELLIGENCE SUMMARY
(Erase heading not required.)

Instructions regarding War Diaries and Intelligence Summaries are contained in F. S. Regs., Part II. and the Staff Manual respectively. Title pages will be prepared in manuscript.

Place	Date	Hour	Summary of Events and Information	Remarks and references to Appendices
MEAULT	12th & 13th		MEAULTE – Quiet day.	
	13th			
	14th		In the trenches – 3 guns Nº 2 section in reserve in MEAULT – note whole time there a quiet period except for fairly heavy shelling at times – two casualties in the Company, one very slight, the more seriously wounded –	
	15th			
	16th			
	17th		A considerable amount of work was done including the entirely new emplacement which is a great success, and is in an excellent position –	
	18th			
	19th		Weather perfect –	
	20th		Considerable aeroplane activity (chiefly our own) – two enemy planes reported to have been brought down in the vicinity –	
	21st			
	22nd		Relieved by 62nd MGC G.Y by 11 A.M. – Company then marched back to VILLE where the night was spent.	
VILLE	23rd	8.30 A.M	Left VILLE and marched to LA NEUVILLE arriving at about 11.30 A.M. fairly good billets provided – great difficulty re-sanitation as there are so many troops in the neighbourhood	
LA NEUVILLE	24th to 30th		Usual programme of training carried out – there is an excellent range near	

T.J.134. Wt. W708–776. 500,000. 4/15. Sir J. C. & S.

Army Form C. 2118.

WAR DIARY
or
~~INTELLIGENCE SUMMARY.~~
(Erase heading not required.)

Place	Date	Hour	Summary of Events and Information	Remarks and references to Appendices
LA NEUVILLE			This place and the Company has not extracted firing, stoppages etc which was a most excellent thing for the general efficiency of the men. A voluntary transport class was formed of some 20 NCOs & men - Transport work was learnt and the men taught as far as possible to ride & look after animals. Several Infantry drill parades were carried out - & most necessary thing as when men come out of trenches discipline is not so good as trained as it really should be. On the whole the period in billets was a great success.	
	31st	9am	GOC 2nd Divn inspected the whole Brigade - an attack was carried out at 10.30 am by the Brigade which was certainly instructive.	

W.A Coldwell Major
OC 63 Machine Gun Coy

Vol 4
63 M G Coy
June 1916.

WAR DIARY or INTELLIGENCE SUMMARY.

Place	Date	Hour	Summary of Events and Information	Remarks and references to Appendices
LA NEUVILLE	June 2nd	7.30 AM	Paraded, moved off 8 AM marched to VILLE arriving 11 AM. Billets inspected, five cleared etc.	
VILLE	3rd		Usual Training programme. Def: Drill, heavy gun 10.30 - 11 AM.	
	4th		Sunday. B.S. Paraded Divine Service.	
	5th		Coy paraded to construct a New Shooting at Transport Lines. B.S. looked into for an hour 9 AM. General poor room 5 PM.	
	6th		10-12. 2-4 hrs good work done on Transport Lines. O.C. inspected horses.	
	7th		Heavy rain - more work on Transport Lines	
	8th		Fine rain - more work on Transport lines	
	9th		Work on Transport lines	
	10th		1 Section went to MEAULT went working party on Transport Lines	
	11th		Coy baths.	
	to		Coy marched to trenches, relieving 64 M.G. Coy.	
	20th		A considerable amount of work done in the trenches, particularly in the way of new emplacements. In all been constructed - weather fair, enemy shelling not great - he ordered five done in order not to draw retaliation on our heavy working parties. -	
VILLE & MEAULT	20th		Coy relieved by 62 M.G Coy - Coy marched to VILLE, at 11.30 paraded open	

WAR DIARY
or
INTELLIGENCE SUMMARY

Army Form C. 2118.

63 M.G. Coy.

(Erase heading not required.)

Instructions regarding War Diaries and Intelligence Summaries are contained in F. S. Regs., Part II. and the Staff Manual respectively. Title pages will be prepared in manuscript.

Place	Date	Hour	Summary of Events and Information	Remarks and references to Appendices
VILLE	20th	11.30	after a Co. return marched to LA NEUVILLE arriving 2.30, rather a trying march as the men were very tired.	
LA NEUVILLE	21st		Day devoted to cleaning up generally	
	22nd		Inspection of Coy guns, rifles, kits etc. by O.C. Coy	
	23rd		Usual Training programme - Various practices including "Trench kickups"	
	24th	5.30	Brigade O.C. unit Conference	
			Company Field Day. An attack practised - a very successful day.	
	25th	2.30	Brigade sports	
	26th		Sunday. Coy. baths - much Sx tra kit returns sent to Corps kit dumps	
			Heralded by the timely arrival of many field carts intended for many weeks c/o - address to Div'l Genl. Tradesp C.T. 27/6/16 -	
	27th	9.30AM	left LA NEUVILLE for VILLE, heavy rain - arrived VILLE 2.30 AM	
			Heavy rain - No 3 section in the trenches in posten by 9.30 P.M.	
	28th		Heavy rain - Coy all ready for trenches 4 PM. Branch off 4.30 - Initiated operation	
			completed - Coy transport remained in billets	
	29th		Quiet with. Coy still busied to - locate much traffic - Quiet expect for the 30th	
	30th	4.30 PM	Coy left VILLE billets took up position in trenches No 1, 2 + 4 sections in 100 STREET - No 3 such in PURFLEET	

W.G. McDonald Major
O.C. 63rd M.G. Co.

Army Form C. 348.

MEMORANDUM.

From O.C. 63 Machine Gun Coy

To D.A.G. 3rd Echelon.

From

To

ANSWER.

July 31st 1916.

Here with war diary of above unit for month ending July 31st

b.G. Motterhead Major
(2/ Northamptonshire Regt)
OC 63 Machine Gun Coy

191

27 Feb
63 M.G.C
vol 5

Army Form C. 2118.

WAR DIARY
or
INTELLIGENCE SUMMARY.
(Erase heading not required.)

Instructions regarding War Diaries and Intelligence Summaries are contained in F. S. Regs., Part II. and the Staff Manual respectively. Title pages will be prepared in manuscript.

Place	Date	Hour	Summary of Events and Information	Remarks and references to Appendices
FRICOURT	Jun 30	7.30 p.m.	The Company took up a position in which was one section which was sent into 101 St. The Company was in position by 7.30 p.m.	
	July 1st	7.00 a.m.	During the last ten minutes of the intense bombardment No 3 Section Lyft 101 S.1 for Purfleet (which had left 101 S2 for Purfleet at 6.30 a.m.) took up positions from which fire could be brought in enfilade and oblique upon the German front line and supports, also upon Taxus Farm and the enemy of this sector matter S/R. Regiment right of a heavy fire upon the German front trenches and supports. The infantry in attacking this trench (Empress Line) encountered fierce opposition and No 3 Section were able to inflict considerable casualties upon the Germans massing in during the second attack upon it until the trench was actually occupied by our troops at about 10.30 a.m. Meanwhile his gun of No 2 Section under 2/Lt Bonellus assisted at 7:30 a.m. in rear of the 4th Battalion Middlesex Regiment who were suddenly marching in fours from the German lines in many cases the gun to Purfleet. 2/Lt Bonellus set many of the gun teams the height. This ½ Section had two guns in action in advance in rear of the 4th Middlesex Regt and to cover the position at about X.27.C.92.3. Showers of crumps made it impossible to do this as the advancing regiment had failed to obtain the first line of German, although they had advanced over it. There were then given to 2/Lt Cragger to take the ½ section forward and to flare up a position from which he could shoot our right Flank. 2/Lt Cragger acting upon these orders crossed to the German lines arriving at Balham, having lost one gun safely over on his own were to the officer over left crossing in Balham. W/Cragger and his ½ Section were still being open and Express Support the general direction of his Majesty but cause what the enemy was however of little effect.	

T.J161. Wt. W708-776. 500,000. 4/15. Sir J.C. & S.

Army Form C. 2118.

63 Machine Gun Coy.

WAR DIARY
or
INTELLIGENCE SUMMARY.
(Erase heading not required.)

Place	Date	Hour	Summary of Events and Information	Remarks and references to Appendices
FRICOURT	July 1st		In day no officer with our own infantry in the trenches 2/Lt Cooper organised a small bombing party & eventually managed to clear Crawl. & Empress Support as far as its junction with Lonely Lane, shooting & bombing several Germans himself with unexpected gallantry. 2/Lt Cooper was then able to move his gun along Dart Lane in conjunction with our own infantry (a mixture of Northumberland Fusiliers and 8th Batt. Lincolnshire Regiment). He succeeded in managing both guns at about X27 c 4 6 being the west boundary of Lincoln Road. From this position he was able to almost enfilade King's Support trench until prevented	
		11.30 am	from firing by the advance of our own infantry. Some about 11.30 AM. He was then able to bring considerable fire to bear on Germans advancing from Lincoln Road across the open & also in a very shallow trench (Bell Lane) causing considerable casualties. At about 2 p.m. 2/Lt Cooper advanced down Gorge Alley but was unable to get to Sunken Road as there was considerable bombing activity at the east end of the trench. He accordingly took up a position about X27 c 5 9 & 63 9 in conjunction with the Lincolnshire Regt. & 63rd Lancaster Regt. where he remained with his guns during the night (July 1st—2nd).	
		12.30 p.m.	Meanwhile 2/Lt Hayward was given orders to advance with 4 guns from Purfleet to the junction of Bon-Accord St with Shaftesbury St to consult the Gunners but as soon as practicable with his guns (June 12.30 p.m.) He defended further on right flank from Lincoln Road and to take up his position in Dart Lane. These orders were carried out though unfortunately his gun teams out of the 4 in west along Rose Avenue were eventually relied on and in support at the junction of Bon-Accord St & Shaftesbury Lane where they came under considerable	
		7 p.m.	shellfire. 2/Lt Hayward with 2 guns took up a position at about X27 c 38 and X27 c 39 arriving there about 7 p.m.	

WAR DIARY or INTELLIGENCE SUMMARY.

(Erase heading not required.)

Army Form C. 2118.

63 Machine Gun Coy

Instructions regarding War Diaries and Intelligence Summaries are contained in F. S. Regs., Part II. and the Staff Manual respectively. Title pages will be prepared in manuscript.

Place	Date	Hour	Summary of Events and Information	Remarks and references to Appendices
FRICOURT	July 1st		From this point it was useless to bring a heavy fire to bear upon Fricourt & Fricourt Wood as ordered during the night	
	July 2nd	3.30 am	2/Lt Hayward & Cregor were properly disposed importantly owing to the intense Fricourt & Fricourt Wood of our own infantry. Things were most difficult for up to the German held they moved our guns forward up to sight.	
		10.30 am	At 10.30 a.m. the guns under 2/Lt Hampson at the junction of Bonn Accord St & Shaftesbury were called in & both up to position in 100 d. At 4.30 p.m. the reserve guns in 100 d were moved into Surrey St. They had been extraordinarily immune from shell fire, though many shells fell close to 100 d. 2/Lt Cregor found one abandoned gun which he immediately mounted and manned by new crew who at start had been used to take from Company Head quarters. The remainder of the day proved quietly except for bursts of enemy shell fire.	
	July 3rd		Heavy shelling in the trenches in square X 27 c. 2/Lt Cregor & Hayward who had been instructed to attack themselves to the companies and did what they were situated advance with them confirming some defensive flank facing N.E. & took up positions at X 27 b 29 & X 21 d 38.3 for what fire could be brought to bear on N.E. & E. direction. There	
		4 p.m.	4 p.m. guns were in position by about 4 p.m.	
			Owing to defensive line being taken up, 2 guns were used to take up a position just E of Bellow Rd. there	
		2 p.m.	2 p.m. guns were in position under 2/Lt Hay of no 1 Section by 2 p.m.	
			During the afternoon the Germans paid particular attention in the way of shells to Red Alley & Dingle trench,	

WAR DIARY or INTELLIGENCE SUMMARY

Army Form C. 2118.

63 Machine Gun Coy

(Erase heading not required.)

Instructions regarding War Diaries and Intelligence Summaries are contained in F.S. Regs., Part II. and the Staff Manual respectively. Title pages will be prepared in manuscript.

Place	Date	Hour	Summary of Events and Information	Remarks and references to Appendices
FRICOURT	July 3rd		resulting in the blowing up of 1 gun round of the team of No 3 Section. 2/Lt Hayward however found a gun which was quietly manned by reinforcements sent from Company Headquarters.	
		9.30 p.m.	At 9.30 p.m. orders were issued for the Company to come out of action. All guns accordingly withdrew to D.2 dump at Norfolk Cemetery to await transport.	

Remarks.

Wonderful communication was kept up between O.C. Company & Section Commanders by means of orderlies. Company orderlies was able to largely detail casualties made up of various orderlies sent back by orderly. Section Commanders were instructed to send back by orderly their exact positions when they advanced. This was well carried out and proved very successful indeed. In the night 1 July 1916 2/Lt Farr (in reserve) with a party of 20 men & 1 N.C.O. managed to carry up various stores to the infantry in the firing line. This officer showed a marked ability in finding his way about strange trenches in a most direct manner with no loss of time.

Remarks re transport

A. In case of a general advance of the 63rd Inf Bde. either S.A.A. boxes or rations would have had to be forsaken owing to lack of transport, as gun limbers had to be used for the carrying of rations. Two extra limbers would be an enormous advantage. This is a most important question.

B. It is most important that the Company should have an extra officer whose duties are connected purely with transport matters. & this case an officer had to be taken from his section in order to attend to the Company transport.

Army Form C. 2118.

WAR DIARY
or
INTELLIGENCE SUMMARY. 63 Machine Gun Coy
(Erase heading not required.)

Instructions regarding War Diaries and Intelligence Summaries are contained in F. S. Regs, Part II. and the Staff Manual respectively. Title pages will be prepared in manuscript.

Place	Date	Hour	Summary of Events and Information	Remarks and references to Appendices
FRICOURT	July 4th	1 AM	Company marched to DERNANCOURT, where billets were provided	
DERNANCOURT	5th	9 AM	Coy entrained & detrained at SAILLY Sur SOMME, arriving about noon - marched to VAUX	
VAUX	5th	2 PM	Transport following by road arrived about 8 PM -	
"	6th		Thorough overhauling of Guns - Equipment - Stores etc -	
"			Limbers cleaned etc - Coy rested - Draft of some 30 men arrived - They appear good men -	
"	7th	4 PM	Coy marched with Brigade to TALMAS - Where billets were found for the night	
"	8th	8 AM	Coy moved with Brigade to PAS and Halte at GRENAS - marching by the road	
GRENAS			POCHEVILLERS MARIEUX THIÈVRES FAMECHON - arriving GRENAS 4.45 PM -	
"	9th			
"	10th		O.C. Coy visited trenches in the neighbourhood of BIENVILLERS -	
			Coy memorial service 5 PM	
GRENAS	11th	9 AM	Coy marched with Brigade via GRINCOURT - GAUDIEMPRE - HUMBERCAMP - POMMIER to BIENVILLERS - arriving about 4 PM. Visited the emplacements in the line -	
			Trenches in very bad condition - an enormous amount of work & redistribution of guns	
			to be done -	
BIENVILLERS	12th		New emplacements chosen by O.C. Coy -	

Army Form C. 2118.

WAR DIARY
or
INTELLIGENCE SUMMARY.
(Erase heading not required.)

63 Machine Gun Coy.

Place	Date	Hour	Summary of Events and Information	Remarks and references to Appendices
BIENVILLERS	15th Feb.		Two new Emplacements chosen – 7 guns moved accordingly. One gun extended throughout the night & early hours of 13/14th. gun also being relieved – This done to attract enemy attention whilst an attack further NORTH is to be carried out –	
"	14th Feb.		Coy. to be relieved – much took has been done in the two days in the trenches – personally I should like the Coy. in a trenches another week as much work remains being to be the adequate defence of the line – with machine guns which can not been seen thoroughly from into seriously in this sector previously – An enormous amount of moving is necessary. Relief complete 8.15 pm. – Coy. marched to HUMBERCAMP	
HUMBERCAMP	15th Feb.	8.30	Brigade march to BERLENCOURT via SAULTY – SOMBRIN – GRAND RULLECOURT – LIENCOURT – Coy. arrived in billets 5.30 at HOUVIGNEUL – The absence of a field cooker is very much felt in the Coy – on days where much marching is in progress – the men have trouble shift but need relieves – which they want get a proper dinner from their cookers at the dinner halt. The strength of the Coy. is over 200 & thus would obviously qualify it for a field cooker.	

T/134. Wt. W708–776. 500000. 4/15. Sir J. C. & S.

WAR DIARY or INTELLIGENCE SUMMARY

Army Form C. 2118.

63 Machine Gun Coy

Place	Date	Hour	Summary of Events and Information	Remarks and references to Appendices
MOYENNEVILLE	16th	9.50 am	2nd owing to KWO establishment (i.e. Coy to be 150 all ranks) & broken Car not to be claimed — This seems hardly fair — possibly it will be rectified later on — Coy passed Brigade starting point. Marched with the Brigade to LE QUESNEL — The line difficult to discern during the march — Rest — MAGNICOURT SUR CANCHE — GOUY EN TERNOIS — A very hot day — unfortunately on arrival in billets at GOUESTREVILLE the Meat had turned consequently the Coy had no meat ration after a hard days marching —	
GOUESTREVILLE	17th	9.30 am	Coy employed cleaning guns — kit etc & resting — storing of mules nearly completed — About that spare kit left at LA NEUVILLE - bag, armr — (spare kit — RANGEFINDERS — SIEGE LANTERNS — TRENCH MOUNTINGS etc.) — We not been told Coy to be carried with no present limited transport at present — Vehicles is missing from one place to another limbers have had trouble this journeys — also is possible at times to find extraneous movements which is to foresee it will be impossible — A baggage wagon is very much needed as the Coy only has 1 supply wagon — No baggage wagon — visit from G.O.C. 63rd Inf Brigade	
"	18th	4.50 pm	Operation Orders to move to VILLERS CAMBLIGNEUL with Brigade	

Army Form C. 2118.

63 Machine Gun Coy

WAR DIARY
or
INTELLIGENCE SUMMARY.
(Erase heading not required.)

Instructions regarding War Diaries and Intelligence Summaries are contained in F.S. Regs., Part II. and the Staff Manual respectively. Title pages will be prepared in manuscript.

Place	Date	Hour	Summary of Events and Information	Remarks and references to Appendices
QUESTREVILLE	18	9.50 am	Coy joined Brigade at X Rds just N.of QUESTREVILLE. marched via 1.50 pm. VILLERS BRULIN – MINGOVAL – billetted with Bde. at CHATEAU DE LA HAIE –	
CHATEAU DE LA HAIE	"		Men have been such an accumulation of months of filth –	
"	"	6. pm	Billets cleared & also neighbouring unoccupied billets and fronts thus in –	
"	19th	9 am to 12.30 pm	Guns, harness, limbers, rolls equipment etc throughly cleaned – Coy bathed –	
"	20th	10.55 am	G.O.C. 37th Division inspected Coy first line transport, which was inspected strict. Considering the recent marching etc –	
			visual programme of work Foreseen for Gunners –	
"		2.30 pm	T.C. Coy etc. visited interesting line of trenches behind SOUCHEZ –	
"	21st	9 am to unsteadily 11 am	Infantry Drill – a good hard parade which has done much good – Machine Gunners should be filled at Infantry Drill etc. Rev Ken Infantry –	
		11.30-12.30	Cleaning of guns etc	
		2-4	Coy marched thru Chick. Lochs, trials of Lewis section arrangement –	
			G.O.C. of Army Reinforced Brigade – cancelled – unfortunately as he was ready for him	
"	22nd	9-11.30	Physical Training – ½ hour Infantry Drill with good results – Machine men instr.Officers –	
		2-3 pm	Lecture on discipline by section officers –	

Army Form C. 2118.

WAR DIARY
or
INTELLIGENCE SUMMARY.
(Erase heading not required.)

63 Machine Gun Coy

Instructions regarding War Diaries and Intelligence Summaries are contained in F. S. Regs., Part II. and the Staff Manual respectively. Title pages will be prepared in manuscript.

Place	Date	Hour	Summary of Events and Information	Remarks and references to Appendices
CHATEAU DE LA HAYE	23rd		Church Parade 12 noon. Orders to put guns into the BAJOLE & BAJOLE No 3 decep T.S. / No 2 fort in other position. Switch line - this to be carried out during the afternoon - Relief completed by 4.30 PM.	
	24th		Orders to relieve the 140th M.G. Coy on the 25th.	
	25th		Relief completed by midnight - 3 sections being in the line, 1 in reserve.	
CAMBLAIN L'ABBE	26th		Coy H.Q. moved to CAMBLAIN L'ABBE which own team 140 E M.G. Coy - Coy's transport line being at MAISNIL BOUCHE - The line seems well adapted for the use of Machine Guns - Most Gun positions being able to command the N. slopes of the VIMY RIDGE in case of hostile attack, & also giving a good line of fire of these gun positions sweeping the ZOUAVE VALLEY. Good any rate to most of the gun positions which is an essential to a gun position, the gun teams & guns being distributed during a heavy bombardment & able to carry out & be dug out to repel an attack at the critical moment. One would like much R.E. labour to assist in constructing dug outs when necessary. Men will no doubt be more readily provided when the true use of Machine Guns is more appreciated. Unfortunately, most merchants can be seen by the Germans behind our line owing to the fact that the PIMPLE on the N end of the VIMY RIDGE is in their hands - this in turn is however commanded by the LORETTE RIDGE which happily is in our hands.	

T2134. Wt. W708-776. 500000. 4/15. Sir J. C. & S.

Army Form C. 2118.

WAR DIARY
or
INTELLIGENCE SUMMARY.   63 M.G.Coy
(Erase heading not required.)

Instructions regarding War Diaries and Intelligence Summaries are contained in F. S. Regs., Part II. and the Staff Manual respectively. Title pages will be prepared in manuscript.

Place	Date	Hour	Summary of Events and Information	Remarks and references to Appendices
COMBLAIN L'ABBE	27th	2pm.	Coy HQ moves to the trenches to CABARET ROUGE. Transport left at MAISNIL BOUCHE	
CABARET ROUGE	28th		Coy. Dispose of CAMBLAIN L'ABBE - + 1 Section. Much work done in improving existing emplacements. Reconnoitering day and night, making of proper latrines - Barrage where looked out from German 2nd line trenches in case of attack from me to keep at night.	
	29th 30th 31st		Indirect fire carried out by 2 reserve guns in Coy H.Q. on the night of 29th & 30th. Line is not as yet in position occurred in satisfactory condition - Appears in not pleasant owing to the existence of so many of our own dead Germans.	

W.A. Coldwell Major
O.C. 63rd M.G. Company

www.ingramcontent.com/pod-product-compliance
Lightning Source LLC
Chambersburg PA
CBHW081249170426
43191CB00037B/2099